LIFE IN
A VICTORIAN
WORKHOUSE

FROM 1834 TO 1930

PETER HIGGINBOTHAM

IMPORTANT DATES

1536 Dissolution of the monasteries begins – religious houses provided for the poor.

1601 The Poor Relief Act makes parishes responsible for poor relief in England and Wales.

1795 The 'Speenhamland system' links labourers' minimum wages to the price of bread.

1834 The Poor Law Amendment Act creates a new poor relief system based on union workhouses.

1837 Civil registration of births, marriages and deaths begins, administered by Poor Law Unions.

1838 The Irish Poor Relief Act introduces the union workhouse system into Ireland.

1842 Some unions allowed to give 'out relief' to able-bodied men in return for work.

1845 The Scottish Poor Law Act passed. Start of the Great Famine in Ireland. A scandal erupts over conditions at the Andover workhouse.

1847 The Poor Law Commissioners replaced by the Poor Law Board. Married couples over the age of 60 in a workhouse can request a shared bedroom.

1867 The Metropolitan Asylums Board created to provide care for London's paupers with infectious diseases or mental impairment.

1871 The Poor Law Board replaced by the Local Government Board.

1900 A major overhaul of workhouse diets implemented.

1905 A Royal Commission appointed to review the poor relief system.

1909 Old Age Pensions introduced for the over-70s. The 1905 Royal Commission's reports published.

1913 Workhouses become officially known as Poor Law Institutions. Children to be removed from workhouses by 1915.

1919 Poor relief administration passes from the Local Government Board to the Ministry of Health.

1930 The Local Government Act abolishes existing poor law authorities. Local councils now administer 'Public Assistance'.

1948 The National Health Service Act comes into operation on 5 July.

The Victorian workhouse is an institution whose powerful image lingers on deep in the minds of many people in Britain, even those born long after it was officially abolished more than 80 years ago. Why should this be? As this guide reveals, the workhouse touched many lives. For those inside the workhouse, entering its doors carried an enormous social stigma that today is hard to imagine. For the elderly, the workhouse gained a reputation as a place that you never came out of – except in a coffin for burial in an unmarked pauper's grave.

A very large proportion of the population had some kind of connection with the workhouse. If they were not living inside it, they were paying for it through the poor rates, supplying it with goods, or buying the firewood the inmates had chopped.

The workhouse was also a highly popular subject for artists, poets, journalists and novelists, most notably in Charles Dickens' tale of workhouse boy Oliver Twist, first published in 1837, the year that Queen Victoria came to the throne. What went on behind the doors of the workhouse held such a fascination for the Victorians that a whole succession of middle-class 'social explorers' clothed themselves in dirty old rags to gain admission for a night's stay and to witness conditions for themselves.

- But what was the workhouse really like?
- Who were its inmates?
- Why and how did they enter the workhouse?
- How did they spend their time?
- How did they ever get out?
- When did the workhouses close?
- And what happened to the buildings?

To these, and many more questions, this guide provides the answers.

▼ The women's day room of St James' parish workhouse on Poland Street in Westminster, drawn c.1809 by Thomas Rowlandson. Parish workhouses were swept away in 1834 by a new poor relief system based on the inhospitable union workhouse – an institution which overshadowed the lives of the Victorian poor.

ORIGINS OF THE VICTORIAN WORKHOUSE

Before their dissolution by Henry VIII in the 1530s, England's monasteries and religious houses had long provided help for the poor, the elderly and the sick. In the decades that followed, the burden of assisting such people was increasingly placed on the better-off members of the community, the landowners and householders. In 1601, the Poor Relief Act formalized how the poor were now to be provided for.

The system adopted, often known as the Old Poor Law, revolved around the parish, the area served by a single priest and his church. Every householder was required to contribute to the poor rate, an annual tax based on the value of their property. The poor rate was mostly distributed as 'out-relief' – handouts to individuals as money, food, clothing or fuel. The 'undeserving' able-bodied poor were expected to work in return for poor relief, with stocks of materials such as wool or flax being bought for this purpose. The poor rate could also be spent on housing the so-called 'impotent poor' – the old, the lame, the blind – who could not work.

The 1601 Act did not mention workhouses, as the term was not yet in general use. Over the next century, however, the idea evolved of a place that accommodated the destitute and required work in return. By the 1770s, almost one in seven parishes was running a workhouse, almost 2,000 nationwide. Many parishes found that workhouses saved them money. There were economies of scale in housing all the parish paupers under one roof. In addition, removing the option of out-relief and offering only the workhouse – the so-called 'workhouse test' – often resulted in many fewer claimants.

Despite the widespread use of workhouses, most poor-rate expenditure remained on out-relief. It further increased in the 1790s when many parishes adopted the 'Speenhamland system' of topping-up low wages in line with the price of bread. With the end of the Napoleonic Wars in 1815, and the introduction of the Corn Laws, the number of poor relief claimants rose sharply, as did the cost of feeding them. In 1818, the national poor rate bill reached a record high, with many people believing that 'living off the parish' was now seen as an easy option by the workshy.

A complete overhaul of poor relief administration came with the 1834 Poor Law

◄ Richard Oastler was one of the leading opponents of the New Poor Law in the north of England. The scroll in his hand demands 'No Bastiles' (bastile was another term for the workhouse) and also mentions the 'Ten Hours Bill', Oastler's campaign to limit the hours worked by children in textile mills.

Amendment Act, often known as the New Poor Law. The new system was centred on the workhouse and aimed to abolish out-relief, at least for able-bodied men, while still providing a safety net for those in genuine need such as the elderly, the sick, and parentless children.

The Poor Law Commissioners, the central body running the new scheme, divided the country up into groups of parishes known as poor law unions. The ratepayers in each union elected a Board of Guardians to manage it locally. Every union was required to set up a union workhouse which would provide only the most basic level of comfort. Offering the workhouse as the only option – the workhouse test – was intended to deter the undeserving poor, with life outside always being more attractive, even for the lowest of labourers scraping by on meagre wages. Grim and forbidding, the Victorian workhouse had arrived.

> ANNO QUARTO & QUINTO
>
> # GULIELMI IV. Regis.
>
> ## CAP. LXXVI.
>
> An Act for the Amendment and better Administration of the Laws relating to the Poor in *England* and *Wales*. [14th *August* 1834.]
>
> WHEREAS it is expedient to alter and amend the Laws relating to the Relief of poor Persons in *England* and *Wales*: Be it therefore enacted by the King's most Excellent Majesty, by and with the Advice and Consent of the Lords Spiritual and Tem-

▲ The opening section of the 1834 Poor Law Amendment Act, one of the most important pieces of British social legislation in the 19th century.

▼ A 17th-century poor box from a church in Buckinghamshire, originally used to collect poor relief contributions.

◄ In August 1842, the newly opened Stockport Union workhouse was attacked and looted by a mob of unemployed workers during an industrial slump.

IN FAVOUR OF 'THE DOLE'

In northern England and parts of Wales, there was considerable resistance to the New Poor Law. Northern manufacturing districts such as East Lancashire and West Yorkshire often viewed workhouses as ineffective, either standing empty in good times or overwhelmed by claimants in periods of downturn. Employers preferred to give short-term handouts or 'dole', allowing families to stay in their own homes and get by until conditions improved. In towns such as Bradford and Huddersfield, opposition sometimes resulted in physical attacks on poor law officials and running battles with army troops.

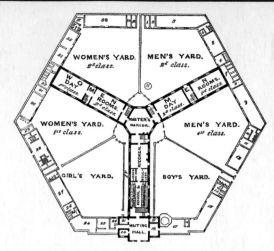

People were not 'sent' to the workhouse – entering it was, in theory at least, a voluntary decision. However, many of those passing through its doors, the elderly, the chronic sick, unmarried mothers-to-be, the mentally impaired, abandoned wives and orphaned children, had no other option. The stigma attached to entering a workhouse, and the fear of never getting out, meant that it was often a last resort.

Entering a workhouse usually involved an initial interview with one of the poor law union's Relieving Officers, who regularly visited designated places in each parish in the union. Applicants for relief would explain their circumstances, probably hoping for an offer of out-relief. If this was refused, an 'offer of the house' was the most likely outcome, with a ticket being provided for the applicant, together with any dependants, to receive admission into the workhouse.

After travelling to the workhouse, which could often involve a walk of five or ten miles, there was a lengthy admission process. New arrivals were usually placed in a reception area known as a receiving ward. Their details were taken, their own clothes taken away and put into store, and they would be issued with the workhouse uniform. They were required to take a bath – for

⋀ The ground-floor layout of a 'Y-plan' or hexagonal workhouse showing the separate sections for different categories of inmate. The label 'first class' referred to the elderly and infirm and 'second class' to the able-bodied.

many this could be a novel experience with the resulting change in the colour of their skin making them barely recognizable! All new workhouse inmates were also required to undergo a medical examination before entering the main workhouse in case they were carrying any infectious disease. Finally, all new admissions had to be formally approved by the Board of Guardians at their next weekly meeting.

One of the most unpopular aspects of entering a workhouse, and part of its deterrent regime, was

the separation of inmates into different 'classes' – male and female, infirm and able-bodied, boys and girls under 16, and children under seven. Apart from concessions made for some contact between mothers and children, the different classes lived in separate sections of the workhouse building and had virtually no contact.

Workhouses were not prisons, however, and inmates could leave at any time after giving a brief period of notice so that their own clothes could be retrieved and administrative formalities carried out. As with entry, families had to leave together so that a man could not abandon his dependants to the care of the union.

Inmates could also, with permission, leave the workhouse for a brief period to try and find work or any other means by which they might be able to support themselves outside. In rural areas, where work was seasonal, workhouse populations generally rose in the winter and fell in the summer. For many, though, particularly the old and infirm, the workhouse might be where they spent the rest of their days. A parliamentary report in 1861 found that of the total adult workhouse population of 67,800 more than 14,000 had been inmates for more than five years.

▲ The Board of Guardians could summon applicants for relief to appear before them. This would no doubt have been an intimidating experience, as illustrated here by the heroine of the 1840s' novel *Jessie Phillips*, shown collapsed on the board-room floor.

◄ The forbidding entrance to the union workhouse at Braintree in Essex. At the left are the porter's lodge and receiving wards, where new arrivals were quarantined before admission.

THE 'INS AND OUTS'

Despite the time-consuming admission and discharge procedures, some paupers entered and left the workhouse with surprising frequency. In 1901, an 81-year-old woman named Julia Blumsun was found to have entered the workhouse on 163 separate occasions during that year alone. Such people – who became known as the 'ins and outs' – were very unpopular with workhouse staff who could do little to prevent such behaviour, until discharge regulations were finally amended in the early 1900s.

◄ Elderly men and women awaiting admission to a London workhouse are provided with a meal by the Church Army, founded in 1882 by the Revd Wilson Carlile to assist the poor and needy.

WORKHOUSE BUILDINGS

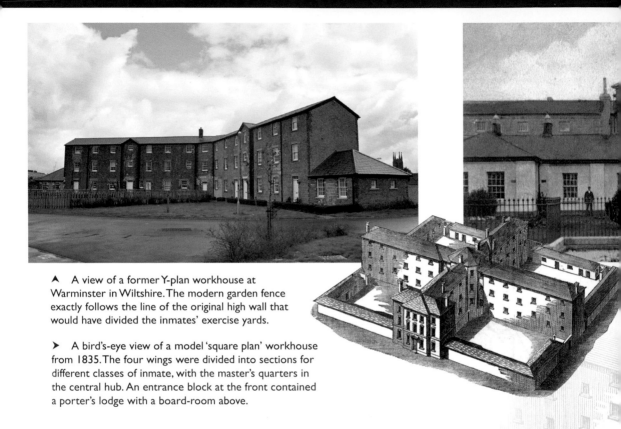

▲ A view of a former Y-plan workhouse at Warminster in Wiltshire. The modern garden fence exactly follows the line of the original high wall that would have divided the inmates' exercise yards.

➤ A bird's-eye view of a model 'square plan' workhouse from 1835. The four wings were divided into sections for different classes of inmate, with the master's quarters in the central hub. An entrance block at the front contained a porter's lodge with a board-room above.

When it came to providing workhouses, unions could either enlarge and adapt existing parish workhouse buildings or erect completely new purpose-built premises. The majority of unions followed the second course, usually erecting their new workhouse towards the edge of the union's main town.

The most important design feature of a workhouse building was its separation of the different categories of inmate. Within the building, doors and staircases were arranged to prevent contact between the various classes, while the outside space was divided up into separate exercise yards by high walls. Each class usually had its own day-room on the ground floor with dormitories located above.

In 1835, to help unions design suitable buildings, the Poor Law Commissioners issued model plans for several different workhouse layouts. Most of

the variations were on the radial principle, popular in prison buildings earlier in the century, with inmates housed in wings connected to a central 'hub'. The three-wing version, in the shape of a 'Y', was also known as the hexagonal layout because of the shape formed by its perimeter outbuildings which might include workshops, stores, a laundry, bakehouse, punishment cell and mortuary. In a similar way, the four-wing version, in the shape of a cross, was also known as the square layout. Both variations included an entrance block, placed at the end of one of the wings, which housed a porter's lodge and the Guardians' board-room. The workhouse master and matron had their quarters in the upper floors of the hub, where windows allowed a clear view over all the inmates' yards.

The one communal area of the workhouse was the dining-hall which often also served a dual

⋏ The union workhouse at Liskeard in Cornwall, opened in 1839, was designed by the eminent Victorian architect Sir George Gilbert Scott and his partner William Bonython Moffatt. Scott and Moffatt eventually designed over 40 workhouses.

⋏ The imposing main block of the Rochdale Union workhouse in Lancashire, a 'corridor-plan' design from the 1870s which was influenced by the then popular Italianate style of architecture. The central tower concealed a large water tank.

purpose as the chapel. Segregation still operated, however, with different seating areas for the various classes of inmate, sometimes with a central screen separating the men and women.

Later workhouse buildings moved away from the radial layout. Corridor-plan designs became popular in the 1840s where the building comprised a number of long parallel blocks, each having a central corridor with rooms opening off to each side. From the 1870s, there was a move towards pavilion-plan layouts with separate blocks being used for each category of inmate or for other specific purposes. Early union workhouses were often very plain, again reflecting the deterrent character that they aimed to project. As time went on, more decoration was gradually introduced with buildings often reflecting architectural fashions of the day.

For those unions upgrading existing buildings, one option was to deploy different sites for different categories of inmate. The Petworth union in Sussex retained three former parish workhouses:

Petworth (for able-bodied adults), Wisborough Green (for children), and Kirdford (for the old and infirm). However, most unions decided that it was cheaper and more efficient to have a single large establishment. This was particularly true when it came to whole families entering or leaving the workhouse who would otherwise have to be ferried backwards and forwards to the various sites.

Union workhouses varied greatly in size. The tiny Belford workhouse in Northumberland had a capacity of just 30, while the largest in the country, Liverpool, could house a hundred times that number – over 3,000 inmates. Workhouses also differed widely in their facilities. The new Hunslet union workhouse which began construction in 1900 boasted central heating, electric lighting and lifts, automated boiler stokers, and 19 telephone extensions. At the Great Ouseburn workhouse in West Yorkshire in 1930, water was still drawn from wells, heating was mostly by open fires, and electricity came from a paraffin engine.

The workhouse daily routine was one of early rising and early bedtimes, with the hours in between mostly occupied by work, mealtimes and religious observances.

Workhouse inmates slept in dormitories, usually with the beds packed close together. Uniforms would be stored overnight in baskets placed under each bed. Bed sharing was common up until the 1870s. Children in particular often had very cramped accommodation – in 1838, it was revealed that in part of London's Whitechapel workhouse 104 girls were sleeping four or more to a bed in a room 88 feet (27m) long, 16½ feet (5m) wide and 7 feet (2.1m) high.

Meals were to be eaten with 'order, decorum' and, until 1842, in silence. Communal prayers were read by the workhouse master before breakfast and after supper each day. On Sundays (and also on Good Friday and Christmas Day) work was restricted to essential domestic tasks only. Instead, inmates attended 'Divine Service' in the morning and evening, at which the workhouse chaplain officiated.

Inmates generally washed themselves in water from a bucket or bowl or direct from a hand-pump in one of the yards, although a small washroom – known as a lavatory – could also be provided for this purpose. Baths, if provided, were often of the portable tin variety, with hot water having to be carried in buckets from the workhouse kitchens.

Workhouse life was governed by numerous rules, with penalties for those who broke them. Lesser infringements such as swearing, gambling or failing to work were punishable by up to two days on a bread and potato diet. More serious offences such as assaulting another person or damaging workhouse property could result in a period of solitary confinement in the 'refractory cell' or being sent before a magistrate.

Life inside the workhouse was not entirely devoid of pleasure, however. By the 1890s, most workhouses had a library and a supply of

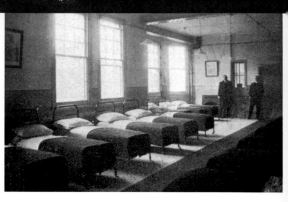

▲ A dormitory at London's St Marylebone workhouse in around 1900. Inmates had no possessions so there was no need for drawers or lockers; their uniforms were stowed in a basket under their beds at night.

SPENDING A PENNY

Workhouse loos were fairly basic. The 'privy' provided one or more seats over a cesspit or tank which was emptied periodically, the contents often then used as manure. In the dormitories, chamber pots might be provided or a communal tub which was carried away and emptied each morning. The earth closet, patented in 1860, deodorized deposits with a sprinkling of dried earth which then produced excellent fertiliser. It proved particularly useful in rural areas or in buildings where no water supply existed. At around the same period, the water closet, with a reservoir of water to flush away deposits, was also gaining popularity. If a workhouse did provide such a luxurious facility, a single water closet would probably serve a very large number of inmates. Workhouse water closets often suffered from poor maintenance and erratic water supplies so could get extremely smelly.

newspapers and magazines. Concerts or other entertainments were sometimes put on, and trips to the country or seaside arranged in the summer. In 1898, inmates of the Haslingden workhouse in Lancashire were treated to a performance from a phonograph, then still a very novel experience.

DAILY TIMETABLE

	Summer	Winter
Rising & roll call	6 a.m.	7 a.m.
Breakfast & prayers	6.30 a.m.	7.30 a.m.
Start work	7 a.m.	8 a.m.
Dinner	12 noon	12 noon
Resume work	1 p.m.	1 p.m.
Supper & prayers	6 p.m.	6 p.m.
Bedtime	8 p.m.	8 p.m.

➤ The daily routine of the workhouse was punctuated by the ringing of its bell to signal the times for work and for meals. This example hung above the workhouse at Stourbridge in Worcestershire.

⋀ When workhouse inmates were not at work, religious services occupied much of their time. In this view of a service being conducted in the open air, men and women are seated separately as usual.

⋁ Uniformed inmates in the workhouse dining hall at Mitcham in Surrey in 1896; male inmates are seated at the back of the room.

ANDOVER SCANDAL

In 1845, an official inquiry was launched after it was revealed that inmates at the Andover workhouse in Hampshire were so hungry that they had been fighting over shreds of rotting meat and marrow left on the bones they had been given for pounding. The resulting scandal led to the banning of the task from workhouses and, ultimately, to the demise of the Poor Law Commissioners.

⋏ The workhouse at Andover which became the centre of a much publicized scandal.

In return for their board and lodging, adult workhouse inmates were required to work six days a week 'according to their capacity and ability' as the regulations put it. The work was unpaid and performed in the workhouse and its grounds; inmates were not sent to work for outside employers.

The women were mainly employed in carrying out the domestic chores of the workhouse. These included the daily cleaning of the workhouse, helping to prepare food in the kitchens, and laundry work. Workhouses generally had a wash-house where the dirty clothing and bed linen were washed, and a separate laundry room where, after being dried, it was ironed and folded. Females were also sometimes employed in making and maintaining the inmates' workhouse uniforms. Other occasional jobs for the women could include nursing in the workhouse infirmary and supervising young children if the workhouse had a nursery.

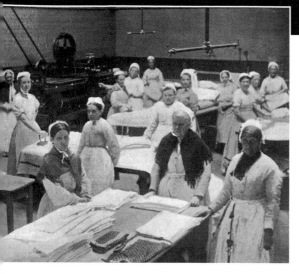

◄ The shoemaking workshop at Mitcham workhouse. Mitcham prided itself on giving its inmates useful work to do rather than tasks such as stone breaking.

Able-bodied men were employed in a wide variety of manual labour tasks. In the early years of the union workhouse, the work was often strenuous but with little practical value and was intended to add to the deterrent character of the institution. Some of the most common tasks of this type were stone breaking, corn grinding, oakum picking and bone crushing.

Stone breaking involved smashing up large lumps of stone with a hammer into pieces small enough to fit through a metal grille. The broken stone could then be sold off for road-making.

Corn grinding involved several men turning a large capstan to rotate a heavy millstone. Oakum picking required the teasing apart of old hemp ropes into their raw fibres which could then be sold for mat-making, or for mixing with tar and used to seal the lining of wooden ships. Bone crushing entailed using a heavy iron 'rammer' to pound old meat bones from the kitchens into dust for use as fertilizer.

Many workhouses, particularly those in rural areas, cultivated the land around the workhouse. This provided both useful work for the inmates and also a supply of vegetables for use in the workhouse. Many workhouses also kept pigs, fattened with waste from the kitchens. For older or less physically able inmates, a common task was the chopping and bundling of wood which could then be sold to people living in the area.

Over the years, the range of work grew wider with increasing use made of any skills that inmates already had. A good illustration of the variety of employment is provided by an 1888 report on the Macclesfield workhouse in Cheshire, which found that amongst the able-bodied females there were: 21 washers, 22 sewers and knitters, 12 scrubbers, 12 assisting women, 4 in the kitchen, 4 in the nursery, and 4 stocking darners. On the men's side there were: 2 joiners, 1 slater, 1 upholsterer, 1 blacksmith, 3 assisting the porter with the tramps, 6 men attending the boilers, 3 attending the stone-shed men, 4 whitewashers, 4 attending the pigs, 2 looking after sanitary matters, 1 regulating the coal supply, 18 potato peelers, 1 messenger, 26 ward men, and 2 doorkeepers.

◄ A group of women engaged in oakum picking where the solid chunks of old rope, visible on the floor, are picked apart into their constituent fibres.

WORKHOUSE FOOD

⋏ Ranks of inmates seated in the dining hall at the St Marylebone workhouse in around 1900. Their plates, clearly containing rather more than bread and cheese, indicate the improvements in food by this time.

⋏ A large party of inmates from the Camberwell workhouse in south-east London, eating their dinner during their annual outing to Bognor Regis. There is a large bottle of beer at each place setting.

The food in a Victorian workhouse was very basic and, like many other features of workhouse life, intended to make life outside seem a more attractive option. In 1835, each workhouse had to adopt one of the six 'dietaries' or weekly meal plans issued by the Poor Law Commissioners.

The main constituent of all workhouse diets was bread, which could either be bought in from a local supplier or, in some places, produced in the workhouse's own bakehouse. At breakfast it was usually supplemented by porridge or gruel (thin porridge). The evening supper again included bread and was generally accompanied by cheese or broth (a soup containing a few vegetables and thickened with barley, rice or oatmeal).

The midday dinner was the meal that varied most, although on several days a week it could again just consist of bread and cheese or broth. Other dinner fare included suet pudding, soup and, just two or three times a week, potatoes and boiled meat such as mutton.

Some concessions were made to the elderly, who might be allowed a small daily ration of butter, tea and sugar. From the age of nine, children generally received the same diet as adult females, while younger children were fed 'at discretion'. From 1856, separate dietaries were introduced for the infirm and for children which included greater allowances of milk and meat.

Will Crooks, a socialist politician from London's East End, spent time in the Poplar workhouse as a child in the 1860s but later rose to become Chairman of the Poplar Board of Guardians. He later recounted how on his first tour of inspection at the workhouse he had found sullen and tearful elderly inmates picking out black specks – what turned out to be rat droppings – from the porridge that they were being fed.

Workhouse food gradually improved and became a little more varied. In 1883, for example, the authorities allowed once-a-week fish dinners to be served in some workhouses for a trial period. Although the experiment was broadly successful, some unions decided not to continue the scheme because of their difficulties in cooking fish in large quantities.

Every inmate received the exact amount of food specified in the dietary, regardless of whether or not they actually wanted their full ration. By the end of the 19th century, a significant proportion of the workhouse population consisted of the elderly and infirm, many of whom were physically unable to consume their daily allocation. As a result, a large quantity of food, particularly bread, was being thrown away. By this time it was also acknowledged that more varied and interesting food would benefit the inmates' health and morale.

Under a new dietary scheme introduced in 1900, workhouses could create their own weekly menus from a selection of around 50 dishes which included such mouth-watering treats as sea pie, Irish stew, pasties, shepherd's pie, meat pudding, fish pie, seed cake, dumplings, fruit pudding, roly-poly pudding and, of course, gruel.

POOR FOOD FOR THE POVERTY STRICKEN

Up until the 1880s, the adulteration of food was widespread – milk could be watered down, flour could have chalk or alum added to it, and oatmeal could be replaced by cheaper but less nutritious barley-meal. The system of tendering for supplies such as bread or milk made workhouses particularly susceptible to food adulteration, since the lowest tender was usually awarded the contract. Workhouse inmates, who had a restricted diet to begin with, were also especially vulnerable to any contamination of what limited food they had.

—	BREAKFAST.		DINNER.			
	Bread.	Gruel.	Cooked Meat.	Potatoes or other Vegetables.	Soup.	Brea
	oz.	pints.	oz.	lb.	pints.	oz.
Men .	8	1½	. .	. .	. .	7
Women	6	1½	. .	. .	. .	6
Men .	8	1½	. .	. .	. .	7
Women	6	1½	. .	. .	. .	6
Men .	8	1½	8	¾	. .	. .
Women	6	1½	6	¾	. .	. .
Men .	8	1½	. .	. .	. .	7
Women	6	1½	. .	. .	. .	6
Men .	8	1½	. .	. .	1½	6

▲ Able-bodied dietary (meal plan) number three – one of the six issued by the Poor Law Commissioners in 1835.

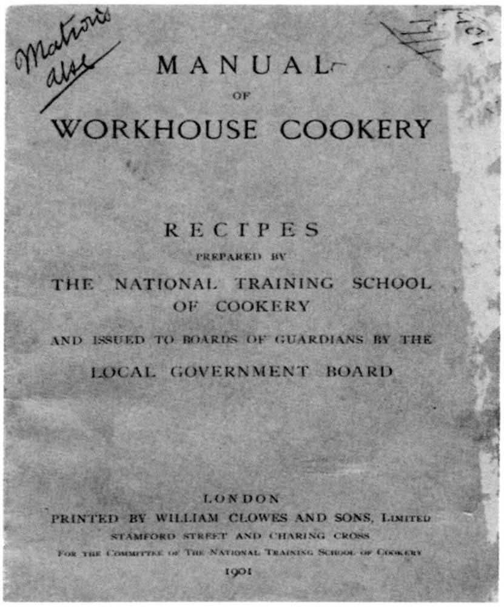
Matron's also

MANUAL

OF

WORKHOUSE COOKERY

RECIPES

PREPARED BY

THE NATIONAL TRAINING SCHOOL OF COOKERY

AND ISSUED TO BOARDS OF GUARDIANS BY THE

LOCAL GOVERNMENT BOARD

LONDON

PRINTED BY WILLIAM CLOWES AND SONS, LIMITED

STAMFORD STREET AND CHARING CROSS

FOR THE COMMITTEE OF THE NATIONAL TRAINING SCHOOL OF COOKERY

1901

▲ The cover of the first-ever official workhouse cookbook, published in 1901 to ensure that all workhouses used the same ingredients, recipes and cooking methods for the food they prepared.

CHILDREN IN THE WORKHOUSE

In 1839, almost half of the country's workhouse inmates were children under the age of 16. Some were part of a family in the workhouse, while others were orphans, or had been deserted, or had parents who could not look after them because of sickness or imprisonment.

Children under three whose mother was in the same workhouse were allowed to live with her. During working hours the children were usually placed in a nursery, typically supervised by an elderly female inmate and with little in the way of toys. Infants aged from three to seven would usually live in the children's section of the workhouse but could sleep in the women's quarters. Those over seven were allowed a daily 'interview' with their parents. However, perhaps to reduce distress all round, a common alternative was a weekly reunion with one or other parent on Sunday afternoons. In 1842, ten-year-old Charles Shaw and his family spent time in Staffordshire's Chell workhouse. He later wrote, 'Sunday afternoon brought an hour of unspeakable joy.'

Workhouses were required to provide three hours of education each day in 'reading, writing, arithmetic, and the principles of the Christian Religion'. Some unions were reluctant to educate pauper children, believing it gave them better treatment than those outside the workhouse. Children breaking workhouse rules could be punished by a reduction in food or a few hours alone in the 'refractory cell'. Boys under 14 could be flogged, but only after two hours had passed since their offence.

There were two aims in dealing with workhouse children. First, to provide them with training to make them employable in later life. For boys, this included trades such as carpentry, boot-making, tailoring or agricultural work, while for girls it meant tasks such as cooking, cleaning or laundering to equip them for domestic service. Second, to house them away from the workhouse and the 'polluting association' with the adult paupers. Over the years, various schemes were developed to try and achieve these goals.

From the 1840s, some unions, particularly in cities such as London and Manchester, set up 'industrial training' schools to house and educate workhouse children. The schools, some holding over a thousand children, were sometimes know as 'barrack schools'. Their critics claimed they were impersonal, expensive to operate, and encouraged the spread of infectious diseases.

Cottage Homes schemes, introduced in the 1870s, were often built as miniature 'villages' in the countryside. They usually included a number of houses, plus a school, infirmary, chapel, and even a swimming pool. In each house a 'family' of 15 to 30 children was supervised by a house mother. The alternative

◄ Children outside the school block at the Shoreditch cottage homes at Hornchurch in Essex. The homes, opened in 1889, were arranged in the style of a village street and included 11 children's cottages, each housing 30 boys or girls.

▼ A group of children and their house mother at the Woolwich Union 'Goldie Leigh' cottage homes. The homes, at Bostall Heath, Plumstead, were erected in 1899 to house pauper children away from the workhouse.

Scattered Homes system instead placed groups of children in ordinary town houses and sent them to local schools.

For orphans and deserted children, a popular option was 'boarding out', what we now call fostering. Unions paid foster parents up to 4s (20p) a week to bring up workhouse children as they would their own. Although occasional cases of ill-treatment or abuse emerged, these were far outweighed by stories of children filled with dread at the possibility of being taken away from the care they received in their foster homes.

Conditions for children still living in workhouses gradually improved. By the 1890s, toys and books were being provided, and there were outings to the country and seaside. However, in 1913 it was officially decreed that no healthy child over the age of three should be resident in any workhouse after 1915.

▼ The vast dining hall at the Central London District School, Hanwell – one of London's large 'barrack schools' for pauper children.

CHARLIE CHAPLIN'S SCHOOLDAYS

In the 1890s, seven-year-old Charlie Chaplin spent some time in a 'barrack school', the Central London District School at Hanwell. He later recalled the school's strict discipline – on Friday mornings, all the boys were lined up to witness the severe canings given to anyone who had stepped out of line.

◄ One of Hanwell school's most famous residents, film star Charlie Chaplin, who stayed at the school from 1896–98. His experience is said to have helped shape his famous 'little tramp' character.

▼ The boot-making workshop at the Kensington and Chelsea cottage homes site at Banstead in Surrey, opened in 1880. Boys at the homes were taught a range of manual crafts which also included carpentry, blacksmithing and plumbing.

Medical care in the mid-Victorian workhouse was often very basic. Every workhouse provided some kind of infirmary for the treatment of sick inmates, but it was often cramped and badly ventilated. Each workhouse was also required to employ a qualified medical officer, although he was frequently poorly paid, and any medicines he prescribed might need to be paid for out of his own salary.

Early nursing care in the union workhouse was usually in the hands of female inmates who would often not be able to read, a serious problem when dealing with labels on medicine bottles. Before 1863, not a single trained nurse was employed in any workhouse infirmary outside London.

In the 1860s, pressure began for improvements in workhouse medical care. Campaigners included nursing pioneer Florence Nightingale, the author Charles Dickens, and Dr Joseph Rogers who had been horrified at the conditions he had found at the Strand Union workhouse in London after becoming its medical officer. Another important contribution came from the medical journal *The Lancet*. In 1865 it began publishing a series of detailed reports about the appalling conditions in London's workhouse infirmaries.

In 1867 the Metropolitan Poor Act was passed, requiring London workhouses to locate their hospital facilities on separate sites from the workhouse.

The Act also led to the creation of the Metropolitan Asylums Board, which took over the provision of much of the medical care for the sick poor in London and set up its own institutions for the treatment of smallpox, fever, tuberculosis and venereal diseases. Florence Nightingale's campaigning also led to improvements in the standard of nursing care with the founding in 1860 of the Nightingale Fund School at London's St Thomas's Hospital.

Workhouse inmates often included a number of those suffering from mental illness or learning difficulties. Although county asylums existed for dealing with such people, many – particularly those who were not disruptive – remained in the workhouse as this was a cheaper option for the union.

Originally, workhouse infirmaries were intended solely for the care of workhouse inmates. From the 1880s, however, admission to workhouse infirmaries was increasingly permitted to those who, though poor, were not sufficiently destitute to require entry to the workhouse. Like all recipients of union relief, such patients first needed to have their means assessed by the union's Relieving Officer and in some cases might be required to contribute towards their maintenance while resident in the infirmary. Prior to 1918, receipt of poor relief disqualified the recipient from voting. The 1885 Medical Relief Disqualification Removal Act recognized the

▼ The massive Holborn Union infirmary, opened in 1879 at Archway in north London, was one of the new generation of separate-site workhouse hospitals established in the last quarter of the 19th century. It later became part of the Whittington Hospital.

◄ Agnes Jones, whose pioneering work at Liverpool workhouse in the 1860s established the use of trained nurses in workhouse infirmaries.

◄ Florence Nightingale's campaigning efforts resulted in the 1867 Metropolitan Poor Act, which led to major improvements in the provision of medical care for London's poor.

AGNES JONES' NURSES

Liverpool pioneered the use of trained nurses in workhouses through an experiment in 1865 funded by local philanthropist William Rathbone. Twelve nurses trained at the Nightingale School were placed under the charge of the workhouse infirmary superintendent, Agnes Jones, whose dedication made the scheme a success. Eventually a skilled nursing system spread to all union infirmaries in the country.

widening of access to workhouse infirmaries and instructed that anyone who was in receipt only of poor-rate-funded medical care no longer lost the right to vote.

The admission of non-paupers to workhouse infirmaries marked the beginnings of Britain's state-funded medical service, providing free treatment for those who would not otherwise be able to afford it. In some workhouses, medical facilities steadily expanded to the point where they outgrew the establishment's role of housing the destitute. When Britain's National Health Service was inaugurated in 1948, a large proportion of its real estate came from former workhouse and poor law establishments.

➤ Wandsworth Union's workhouse infirmary at St John's Hill, Battersea in London, in 1896.

OLD AGE AND DEATH

▲ A Sunday afternoon concert given in 1901 by the National Sunday League at Holborn's City Road workhouse. Some of the audience (and band) appear less than attentive.

Throughout the history of the workhouse, the elderly were always one of the most significant groups of its residents. By 1901, five per cent of the nation's over-65s were living in a workhouse, most of whom would spend the rest of their days there. Perhaps unsurprisingly, entering a workhouse gained a reputation amongst the elderly as a death sentence. There was some truth in this – not because workhouses were such terrible places, but because for many there was nowhere else they could go for nursing or medical care at the very end of their lives.

In fact, conditions for the elderly improved significantly during the Victorian period. This was partly due to the efforts of campaigners such as Louisa Twining who, in 1858, founded the Workhouse Visiting Society after visiting an elderly acquaintance in the Strand Union workhouse. The Society fought to improve the lot of workhouse inmates, particularly the elderly, by providing visitors to those who would otherwise have none, or by reading to those who could no longer read for themselves. Other improvements included the provision of pictures and plants in workhouse wards, and the donation of books and newspapers.

One specific concession to the elderly came in 1847 when married couples over the age of 60 could request a shared bedroom. However, Boards of Guardians made relatively little provision for such accommodation, arguing that elderly couples generally preferred the separation.

Workhouses almost always contained more elderly men than women. Elderly women were usually better at maintaining their independence in the community, while the men were frequently lacking in the most basic household skills – such as cooking and washing – and so ended up needing care.

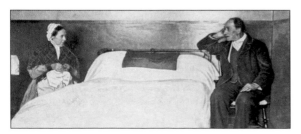

▲ An elderly married couple at the St Marylebone workhouse in their shared bedroom, a concession made to the over-60s in 1847.

▲ Elderly male inmates pass time at the Shipston-on-Stour Union workhouse in Worcestershire.

If an inmate died in the workhouse, the death was notified to their family who could, if they wished, organize a funeral themselves. If this did not happen, which was often the case because of the expense, the Guardians arranged a pauper burial in a local cemetery or burial ground, either in the parish where the workhouse stood, or in the deceased's own parish if they or their relatives had expressed such a wish. A few workhouses had their own burial ground situated on or adjacent to the workhouse site.

The burial would be in the cheapest possible coffin and in an unmarked grave, into which several coffins might be placed on the same occasion. Under the terms of the 1832 Anatomy Act, bodies unclaimed for 48 hours could be donated for use in medical research and training – this was not specific to workhouses, but applied to any institution whose inmates died while in its care. Whatever the fate of the body, deaths were always registered in the normal way.

In September 1883, *The Times* newspaper carried a report about the transport of pauper bodies from Clerkenwell workhouse mortuary by an undertaker's sub-contractor. It had been

➤ Some workhouses had a special coffin for transporting bodies to the cemetery. This one at Londonderry had a hole on top where a warning flag would be placed when the coffin contained a body.

alleged that a coach carrying five coffins, three of adults and two of children, had broken down and the coffins had rolled into the road. It was also claimed that, for the sake of economy, bodies were kept in store until a batch of sufficient size was reached, resulting in offensive smells. The coffins were said to each be identified only by a name chalked on them and that during the journey the writing rubbed off. Although an investigation by a committee of Guardians refuted the allegations, it was agreed that the union should acquire its own hearse, coach and horses for use at pauper funerals.

Pauper funerals were often without mourners. At Bourne in 1901, the workhouse master reported that, despite repeated invitations, workhouse inmates always declined to attend their fellow's funerals. This was perhaps a testimony to the old saying 'rattle his bones, over the stones, he's only a pauper whom nobody owns.'

TRAMPS AND VAGRANTS

Union workhouses originally made no provision for passing tramps and vagrants. In 1837, however, several instances of tramps dying from exposure or starvation after being turned away from the workhouse door resulted in a new regulation, requiring food and a night's shelter to be given to any destitute person in case of 'sudden or urgent necessity', in return for them performing a task of work.

Accommodation for vagrants then became a standard feature of workhouses, usually placed in a separate building near the entrance. These quarters were variously known as tramp or casual wards, with their occupants officially referred to as the 'casual poor', or just 'casuals'. Another term that became popular for the tramps' block was 'the spike', a name whose origins are uncertain but much debated.

The routine for those entering a casual ward began in late afternoon by joining the queue for admission. A spike had only a certain number of beds and latecomers might find themselves turned away. New arrivals would be searched and any money, tobacco or alcohol confiscated. Vagrants would often hide such possessions in a nearby hedge or wall before entering the spike. After being quizzed as to their name, age, occupation, previous stopping place and next destination, entrants had to strip and have a bath – in the same water used by many previous occupants. They were then issued with a blanket and a workhouse nightshirt to wear while their own clothes were washed, dried, fumigated, and stored overnight. Each inmate was given supper, typically eight ounces of bread and a pint of gruel, before being locked up until 6 or 7 a.m. the next morning when a breakfast of bread and tea was provided.

Before being allowed on their way, casuals had to work for up to four hours. Stone breaking and oakum picking were the most common tasks given to men, with cleaning or oakum picking the usual ones for women. From 1882, casuals could be detained for two nights with a whole day's work in between, before being released early on the third day. Casuals were not allowed to return to the same workhouse within 30 days, so many tramps progressed around a circuit of workhouses which were generally a day's walk apart.

Until the 1870s, casual wards had communal dormitories where the inmates either slept in hammocks or on the bare floor. A new form of accommodation then began to be adopted consisting of prison-like cells, usually arranged along both sides of a corridor. Sleeping cells contained a simple bed, usually hinged to fold up against the wall when not in use. Work cells were usually fitted out for stone breaking, typically with a metal grille in the wall through which small lumps of broken stone were passed for collection in the yard outside.

Many tramps had unusual nicknames, as revealed by graffiti collected from the walls of various northern casual wards in 1865:

The York Spinner, Dick Blazeanvy, Lancashire Crab, Dublin Smasher, and Bob Curly called for one night on their road for the tip at Birmingham.

Private notice. Saucy Harry and his moll will be at Chester to eat their Christmas dinner, when they hope Saucer and the fraternity will meet them at the union.

Men queue for admission to the Whitechapel casual ward on Thomas Street in east London in 1902.

TRAMPS' SLANG

Tramps and vagrants had their own slang terms for many things, for example: the 'toby' was the highway; a 'lurk' was a beggar's dodge or performance; 'toke' was bread; 'skilly' was gruel; 'kerbstone twist' was old chews of tobacco; a 'griddler' was a street hymn singer; a 'screever' was a professional writer of begging letters; and 'Lord Nosey' was a casual ward official.

An illustration showing a tramp's stone-breaking cell. The large stones were broken up until the pieces were small enough to pass through the metal grille to the yard outside.

A reconstruction of the tramps' bath at the Guildford 'Spike' in Surrey, one of the very few surviving casual ward buildings and now restored as a workhouse museum.

An example of a communal casual ward where hammock-style beds were slung between the wall and a rail running along the length of the dormitory.

RUNNING THE WORKHOUSE

unning the 600 or so union workhouses in England and Wales was a complex operation. At the centre in London were the Poor Law Commissioners (replaced by the Poor Law Board in 1847, then by the Local Government Board in 1871). The central authorities laid down all the regulations for operating the poor relief system, both within the workhouse and for those receiving relief outside it.

At the local level, each union was run by the Board of Guardians elected annually by the ratepayers. Depending on the union's location, Board members might include local gentry, clergymen, shopkeepers, manufacturers and farmers. The composition of Boards gradually changed over the years, with the first female Guardian being elected in 1875 and an influx of working-class Guardians in the 1890s following a reduction in the property qualification needed for election. The Guardians usually met each week in a board-room at the workhouse and had legal responsibility for the proper operation of the union, especially financial matters. The minutes of the Guardians' meetings were recorded by the union clerk, who also conducted correspondence with the central authorities and prepared any reports that were required.

The workhouse itself was in the charge of the master and matron, usually a married couple, appointed by the Guardians. The master had numerous duties amongst which were 'to enforce industry, order, punctuality and cleanliness', 'to provide work, training or occupation for the inmates', and 'to ensure that the workhouse building, fixtures, fittings etc. are kept clean and in good order'. The matron's duties were largely concerned with the women and children residing in the workhouse, and in the domestic operation of the establishment such as overseeing the kitchen and laundry.

The workhouse porter monitored all the comings and goings at the workhouse and usually had a lodge at the workhouse entrance. He dealt with new entrants arriving at the workhouse, sometimes including those using the casual ward. One of the porter's specific responsibilities was to ensure that no alcohol or other illicit goods were smuggled onto the premises. The porter also helped the master, especially in matters of keeping order amongst the inmates.

Before the state school system began in 1870, many workhouses employed a school mistress and/or master. Apart from the three hours of daily lessons that the children were required to receive,

◄ The master and matron (seated centre) and staff of the Caistor Union workhouse in Lincolnshire in the early 1900s.

workhouse school-teachers were also expected to help their pupils get dressed and washed in the morning, supervise them at meal times, help keep them occupied after lessons, and help put them to bed in the evenings. Perhaps not surprisingly, workhouse teachers often did not stay long in such demanding jobs.

Other workhouse staff, particularly in larger establishments, could include: a cook to oversee the preparation of all the workhouse food; a baker, where the workhouse had its own bakehouse; one or more nurses to attend to the sick in the workhouse infirmary; a laundry supervisor; and a labour master to supervise the inmates' labour and to provide industrial training for the older boys. Other workhouse posts include the relieving officer, chaplain and medical officer.

As well the workhouse's paid staff, the able-bodied inmates contributed to the work of the institution. During the 19th century, the numbers of such inmates gradually declined and workhouses were increasingly forced to hire staff to perform domestic duties. It is interesting to note that the 1881 census for the Wharfedale Union workhouse at Otley in Yorkshire records only two staff in residence, the master and matron, to look after the 85 inmates then in residence.

◄ The Hull Board of Guardians with their chairman wearing his chain of office, at the centre of the front row. Although this view dates from 1912, there is still a notable absence of women on the Board.

Lewes Union.
SCHOOLMISTRESS WANTED.

THE Guardians of the Lewes Union will at their meeting, on Friday, the 16th November, 1877, at ten in the forenoon, proceed to the appointment of a Schoolmistress for the Workhouse children, at a salary of £25 per annum, or such larger sum as the Committee of Council on Education may from time to time award, together with the establishment rations, washing, and apartments in the house.

The person appointed will be required to reside in the School House (detached), and devote her whole time to the care and instruction of the children.

▲ An advertisement, dated 1877, for a resident schoolmistress at the Lewes workhouse in Sussex. The person appointed to the post was expected to devote her 'whole time' (hours not specified) 'to the care and instruction of the children'.

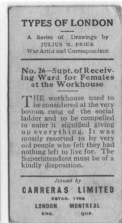

BLACK CAT CIGARETTES

SUPT. OF RECEIVING WARD FOR FEMALES AT THE WORKHOUSE

TYPES OF LONDON

A Series of Drawings by JULIUS M. PRICE War Artist and Correspondent

No. 26—Supt. of Receiving Ward for Females at the Workhouse

THE workhouse used to be considered at the very bottom rung of the social ladder and to be compelled to enter it signified giving up everything. It was mostly resorted to by very old people who felt they had nothing left to live for. The Superintendent must be of a kindly disposition.

Issued by

CARRERAS LIMITED
ESTAB. 1788
LONDON   MONTREAL
ENG.   QUE.

▲ A 'Black Cat' cigarette card illustrating the 'Superintendent of the Receiving Ward for Females' at a large London workhouse. The text notes that she was expected to be of a 'kindly disposition'.

IRELAND AND SCOTLAND

The Irish Poor Relief Act of 1838 introduced the workhouse system to the whole of Ireland along broadly similar lines to that operating in England and Wales and run by the same Poor Law Commissioners. The country was divided up into 130 poor law unions, each run by a Board of Guardians elected every year from the ratepayers, and each required to provide a workhouse. There were, however, some important differences in the Irish system: out-relief was not to be given in any form whatsoever, and clergymen were barred from membership of Boards of Guardians.

English workhouse architect George Wilkinson was appointed to supervise the construction of the new Irish workhouses which, although varying in size, all followed the same basic layout. However, the Commissioners required that the buildings should be 'of the cheapest description compatible with durability… all mere decoration being studiously excluded'. The walls were unplastered and the ground floors made of earth or clay, which was said to be what the inmates would have been used to. The food in Irish workhouses was initially proposed to include just two meals a day, a breakfast of milk and oatmeal 'stirabout', and a dinner of milk and potatoes, again based on what the Irish poor were said to usually eat.

Many Irish workhouses, especially in the west of the country, were slow coming into operation because sufficient funds to pay for their running were not forthcoming from the ratepayers. However, most had opened their doors by 1845, the year in which the Great Famine began to devastate the country. Irish workhouses struggled to meet the starving crowds at their doors, a situation made worse by the subsequent outbreak of diseases such as typhus fever and dysentery. A great number of workhouse inmates perished and were buried in mass graves, with many workhouse staff also dying. The cost of trying to feed the large number of starving poor, and the erection of temporary accommodation and fever hospitals, bankrupted many unions, with many being dissolved for a period and run by paid officials.

▼ The Lewis Combination poorhouse in Scotland's Outer Hebrides, opened in 1896. Some of the poorhouse inmates are just visible along the front of the building.

A Inmates of the Bailieborough workhouse in County Cavan in around 1895. The men are in the workhouse dining hall with their food, probably porridge, being served in a feeding trough containing a portion for each, eaten while standing.

A A re-creation of the scene in the under-roof children's dormitory at the former Londonderry workhouse. The inmates slept on a raised wooden platform and sanitary facilities consisted of a bucket. The building now houses the Derry workhouse and famine museum.

After the famine ended, the Irish workhouse system returned to normality. From the 1850s, the workhouse fever hospitals became increasingly involved in providing medical care to those who were poor but not sufficiently destitute to require entry into the workhouse, something that was not to happen in England and Wales for another 25 years.

◄ A statue in front of the former Roscommon workhouse presents the haunting image of a starving mother and children during the Great Famine in Ireland (1845–50).

During the Irish War of Independence (1919–21) and Civil War (1922–23), many Irish workhouses were occupied by troops, leaving them severely damaged or destroyed. In the newly created Irish Free State (now the Republic of Ireland) the workhouse system was rapidly wound up, while in Northern Ireland it effectively continued operating until 1948.

Scotland's poor relief system, in contrast, was always independent of that in the rest of Britain. The 1845 Scottish Poor Law Act introduced a parish-based poor relief system, administered locally by annually appointed Parochial Boards whose funds could come either from voluntary collections or via a rating scheme. The new poor relief system was overseen by a central advisory body known as the Board of Supervision.

The preference in Scotland was always towards the giving of out-relief rather than through institutional care. However, the 1845 Act allowed large parishes or groups of parishes to set up poorhouses (as the Scottish institutions were usually called) if they wished, with around 70 such poorhouses eventually being established. Like their counterparts in England and Wales, these mainly housed the elderly and the chronic sick. Many smaller parishes also operated parish lodging houses or almshouses where the poor could be housed. The able-bodied were generally excluded from receiving poor relief.

'Please Sir, I want some more' are some of the most well-known words in English fiction and spoken by workhouse inmate Oliver Twist in the novel by Charles Dickens. Although Dickens had visited a number of workhouses, the picture painted in *Oliver Twist* was clearly written for dramatic effect rather than historical accuracy. The story was first published in 1837, precisely at the transition from the parish workhouse era to the new union workhouse system, and contains a rather jumbled mixture of the two. The character of the beadle, for example, was a sort of parish constable who had no role in a union workhouse. Under the new workhouse dietaries issued in 1835, nine-year-old Oliver should have had the same food as an adult female and at least received some bread with his gruel.

The dramatic possibilities of the workhouse attracted many writers during the Victorian period, including Frances Trollope (*Jessie Phillips*), Thomas Hardy (*Far from the Madding Crowd*), George Eliot (*Scenes from Clerical Life*) and John Law (*Captain Lobe*) amongst the best known. Such interest, however, was not restricted to novelists. The workhouse, and those forced through its doors, were a popular subject in poetry, drama, street ballads, art and humour.

In 1879, George R. Sims published *In the Workhouse: Christmas Day*, a dramatic recitation which became hugely popular with Victorian audiences. The verses were an attack on the custom of union Guardians or local gentry, often fur-clad, dispensing largesse at the workhouse Christmas dinners they had funded, a practice some viewed as patronizing.

The 19th-century boom in illustrated weekly magazines also provided a market for workhouse scenes, often giving a very sentimentalized view of their inmates. Two popular exponents were Luke Fildes whose picture *Houseless and Hungry* appeared in the first issue of *The Graphic* magazine in 1869, and Hubert von Herkomer who specialized in

◄ James Greenwood's *A Night in a Workhouse* which caused a sensation on its appearance in the *Pall Mall Gazette* in 1866. The article was then reprinted as a pamphlet whose cover is shown he[re]

CHRISTMAS DA

It is Christmas day in the Workhouse,
 And the cold, bare walls are bright
With garlands of green and holly,
 And the place is a pleasant sight;
For with clean-washed hands and faces,
 In a long and hungry line,

The paupe[r]
 For this [
And the G[
 Altho' the
Have come[
 To watch[

▲ *Applicants for Admission to a Casual Ward* by Luke Fildes. The picture was a reworking of his illustration *Houseless and Hungry*, originally published in *The Graphic*.

▼ A postcard from the early 1900s illustrating the opening stanzas of *In the Workhouse: Christmas Day*.

WORKHOUSE.

es,
line,
ir ladies,

To smile and be condescending,
Put pudding on pauper plates,
To be hosts at the workhouse banquet
They've paid for with the rates.

l wrappers.
ast;

illustrations of the elderly, such as his 1877 *Old Age – a Study* at the Westminster Union, also drawn for *The Graphic*.

Broadside ballads, sold in the streets for a penny or halfpenny, were the popular songs of the day, often anonymous, and were performed in taverns, fairs or in the home. Often set to well-known tunes, the words of the ballads usually commented on topical events of the time. Typical was *The Women Flogger's Lament of Marylebone Workhouse*, published in 1856 following revelations that the workhouse master, Richard Ryan, along with two porters, had been dismissed for whipping female inmates. Perhaps sung to the tune of *Oh Dear, What Can the Matter Be*, it began:

> Oh dear here's a shocking disaster,
> My name is Ryan a poor
>   workhouse master,
> I have now got discharges and my
>   sentence is passed, sirs,
> Because I went flogging the girls.

Life in the 'underworld' presented a fascination for the Victorian middle classes and lurid 'inside' descriptions of institutions such as the workhouse and the spike proved highly popular. These were often compiled by so-called social explorers who disguised themselves as down-and-outs to obtain admission to such places as the casual ward. One of the first undercover reports was *A Night in a Workhouse*, published by James Greenwood in 1866. Greenwood colourfully detailed the repugnant conditions in the Lambeth spike whose much-used bath water he reported as 'disgustingly like weak mutton broth'. His fellow inmates were described as 'towzled, dirty, villainous, they squatted up in their beds, and smoked foul pipes, and sang snatches of horrible songs'. The sensation caused by Greenwood's revelations in turn inspired at least three broadside ballads.

At the start of the 20th century, the increasing numbers of female and working-class Guardians led to pressure for change in the workhouse system. A Royal Commission, appointed in 1905 to review poor relief administration, was famously split in its conclusions. Its Majority Report recommended creating new county-wide poor-law authorities and replacing workhouses with separate and more specialized institutions for children, the old, the unemployed, and the mentally ill. The Minority Report, which emphasized the prevention of destitution rather than its relief, proposed the complete break-up of the poor law system with other authorities providing care for the various groups.

Although no new legislation directly resulted from the Commission's work, a number of improvements did take place in welfare provision. In 1909, the old age pension was introduced for those over 70: 5s (25p) a week for a single person, or 7s 6d (37½p) for a married couple. In 1911 unemployment insurance and health insurance began in a limited form.

In 1913, a complete revision of workhouse regulations took place. The updated version made no mention of the 'workhouse' – the term 'poor law institution' was used instead.

▲ Some of the first recipients of the old age pension in 1909. However, anyone who had received poor relief in the previous 12 months was automatically disqualified from receiving the pension.

Likewise, 'paupers' were instead referred to as 'poor persons'. Within the workhouse, Boards of Guardians could now devise whatever system of inmate classification they felt appropriate.

During the First World War, many workhouses were used as military hospitals or prisoner-of-war camps. Then, in 1919, administration of poor relief passed to the Ministry of Health. The depression following the war, culminating

SMASH UP THE WORKHOUSE.

— BY —

GEORGE LANSBURY, L.C.C.

PUBLISHED BY THE I.L.P. PUBLICATION DEPARTMENT,
30, BLACKFRIARS STREET, MANCHESTER.

⋀ Socialist politician George Lansbury's provocatively titled pamphlet *Smash Up the Workhouse* was published in 1911. Lansbury was a member of the Royal Commission on the Poor Law and an author of its 1909 Minority Report.

in the miners' strike of 1926, put a tremendous strain on the poor-relief system with some unions effectively becoming bankrupt. In 1928, the Minister of Health, Neville Chamberlain, introduced the Local Government Act which would abolish the Boards of Guardians and transfer all their responsibilities to local councils. The Act took effect on 1 April 1930, with many Boards holding sentimental farewell dinners to mark the occasion. At Abingdon in Oxfordshire, the Chairman of the Guardians mourned the imminent closure of the workhouse, hoping that 'all those who have found a refuge from want and trouble will feel the passing of this institution'.

After 1930, some former workhouses were demolished or converted to other uses such as factories, schools and housing. The majority, however, were retained by county councils as Public Assistance Institutions (PAIs) and carried on into the 1930s virtually unaltered from their workhouse days. They inherited the workhouse buildings, many of the same staff, and the same inmates who continued to be the old, the long-term sick, the mentally impaired, unmarried mothers, and vagrants. A few, largely cosmetic, changes were made – the master became known as the superintendent, and uniforms were replaced by 'suitable clothing'.

Even the sweeping changes that came with the launch of the National Health Service (NHS) in 1948 did not completely obliterate the workhouse. Many former PAIs became NHS hospitals but often still carried the stigma from their workhouse days, and were frequently referred to locally as 'the workhouse'. Some of these new hospitals even maintained 'Reception Centres for Wayfarers' – tramps' wards – until the 1960s.

In the 1970s and 1980s, many former workhouse sites were deemed no longer suitable for hospital use and sold off. Many of the old buildings were then refurbished as upmarket residential accommodation whose residents were protected by high walls and electric gates. The former workhouse inmates would no doubt be amazed at how much money their modern counterparts were prepared to pay to be locked in behind the very walls which, in another era, had symbolized so much shame and degradation.

◄ Will Crooks' life was summed up in the title of his biography *From Workhouse to Westminster*; having spent time as a child in the Poplar workhouse, he eventually became a Member of Parliament. As Chairman of the Poplar Board of Guardians, Crooks also fought to improve the help given to the union's poor, in an approach which became known as Poplarism.

▲ Now preserved by the National Trust, the Southwell Union workhouse at Upton was originally opened in 1824. Its strict regime provided a model for the deterrent workhouses of the Victorian era.

▲ The workhouse in Newbury, Berkshire, dating from 1627, one of the oldest surviving workhouse buildings in Britain. This block, now housing a museum, originally formed one side of a quadrangle.

Below is a list of museums housed in former workhouse buildings. Most include displays about their workhouse past. Further information and details of opening times are available on each museum's website.

Gressenhall Farm and Workhouse, Gressenhall, Dereham, Norfolk NR20 4DR; 01362 869263
www.museums.norfolk.gov.uk/default.asp?Document=200.50

Guildford Spike, Warren Road, Guildford, Surrey GU1 3JH; 01483 569944
www.guildfordspike.co.uk

Nidderdale Museum, 5 King Street, Pateley Bridge, North Yorkshire HG3 5LE; 01423 711225
www.nidderdalemuseum.com

Red House Museum, Quay Road, Christchurch, Dorset BH23 1BU; 0845 603 5635
www.hants.gov.uk/redhouse

Ripon Workhouse Museum, Allhallowgate, Ripon, North Yorkshire HG4 1LE; 01765 690799
www.riponmuseums.co.uk/html/workhouse.html

Thackray Medical Museum, 141 Beckett Street, Leeds LS9 7LN; 0113 244 4343
www.thackraymuseum.org

The Workhouse, Southwell, Upton Road, Southwell, Nottinghamshire NG25 0PT; 01636 817 260
www.nationaltrust.org.uk/theworkhouse

Vestry House Museum, Vestry Road, Walthamstow, London E17 9NH; 020 8496 4391
www.walthamforest.gov.uk/rd/vestry-house

Weaver Hall Museum & Workhouse, 162 London Road, Northwich, Cheshire CW9 8AB; 01606 271640
www.cheshirewestandchester.gov.uk/visiting/museums/the_weaver_hall_museum.aspx

Derry Workhouse Museum, 23 Glendermott Road, Waterside, Londonderry, Derry BT47 6BG; 028 7131 8328
www.derrycity.gov.uk/museums/workhouse.asp

Dunfanaghy Workhouse Heritage Centre, Figart, Dunfanaghy, County Donegal, Ireland;
00353 (0)74 9136540
www.dunfanaghyworkhouse.ie

Donaghmore Famine Workhouse Museum, Donaghmore, Portlaoise, County Laois, Ireland; 00353 (0)86 8296685
www.donaghmoremuseum.com

More Information

Extensive information on the history of the workhouse with details of many hundreds of individual workhouses is available on the website: www.workhouses.org.uk.

Information correct at time of going to press.